Your Bones

Amy Hunter

Contents

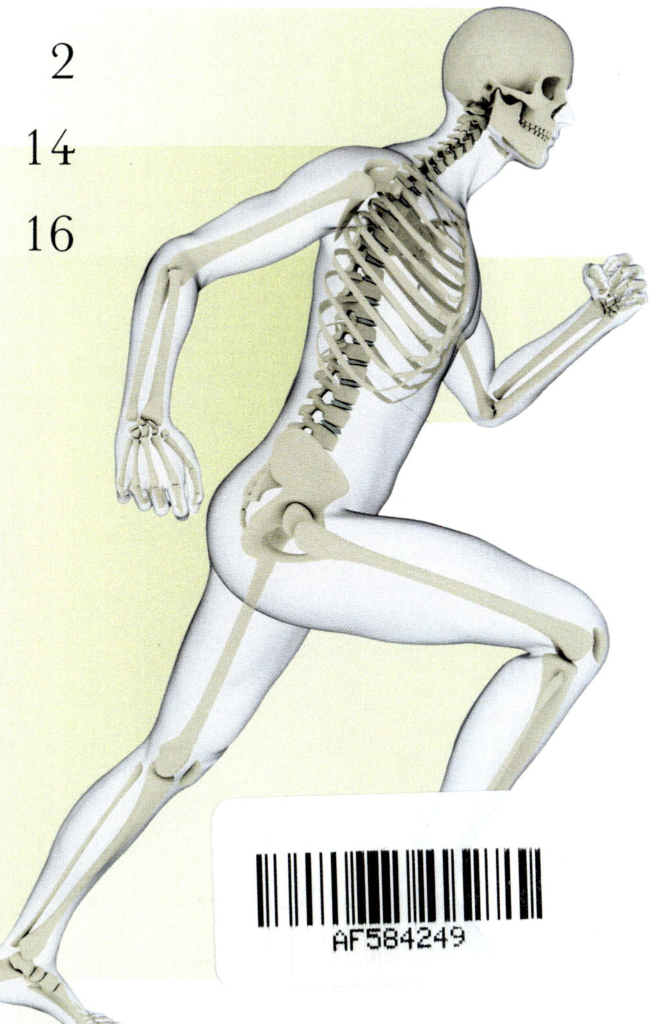

All About Bones

Hello, I'm Skeleton Sam.

I'm here to tell you all about bones!

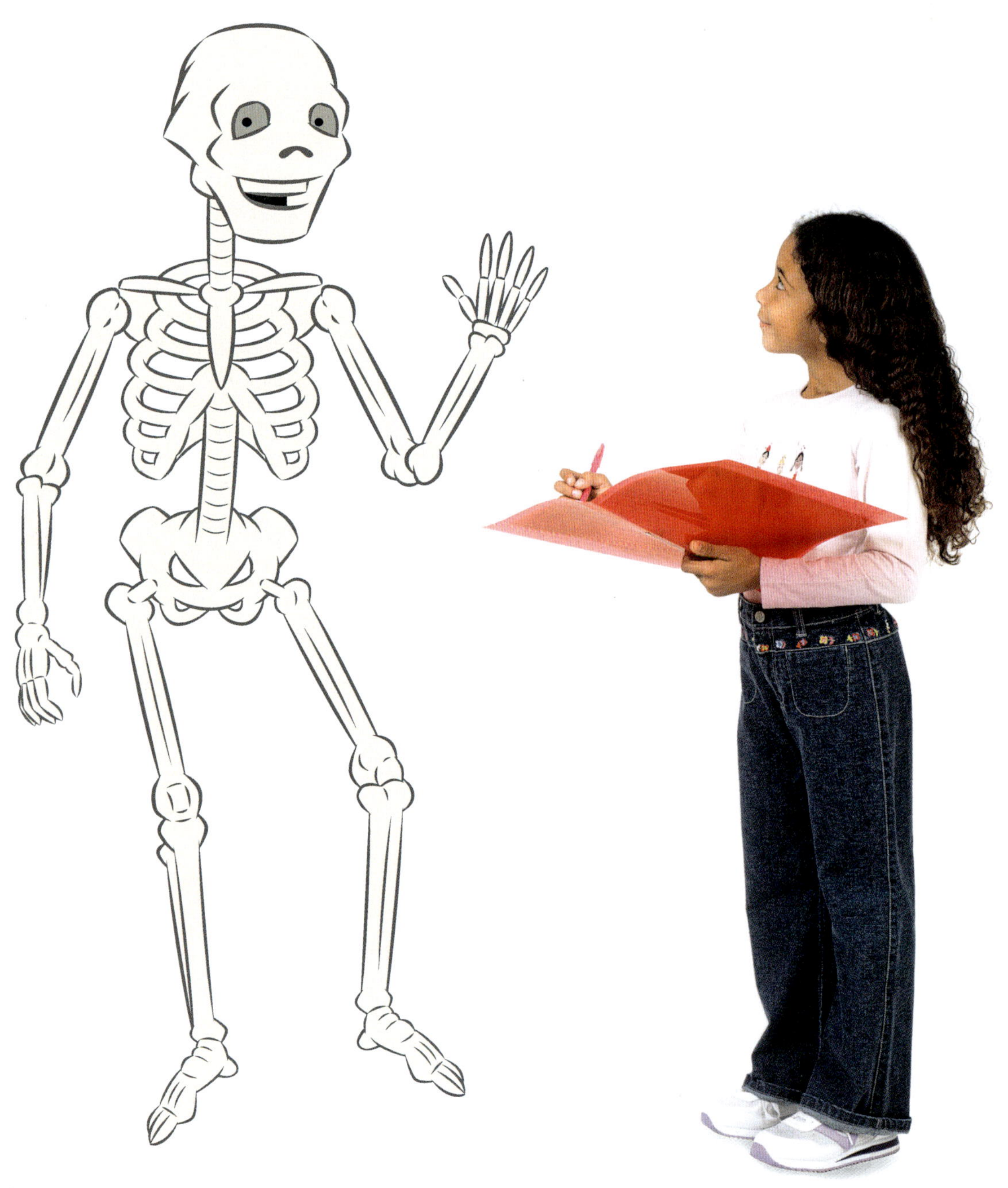

There are lots of bones in your body.
They give your body its shape.
All your bones make up your skeleton.

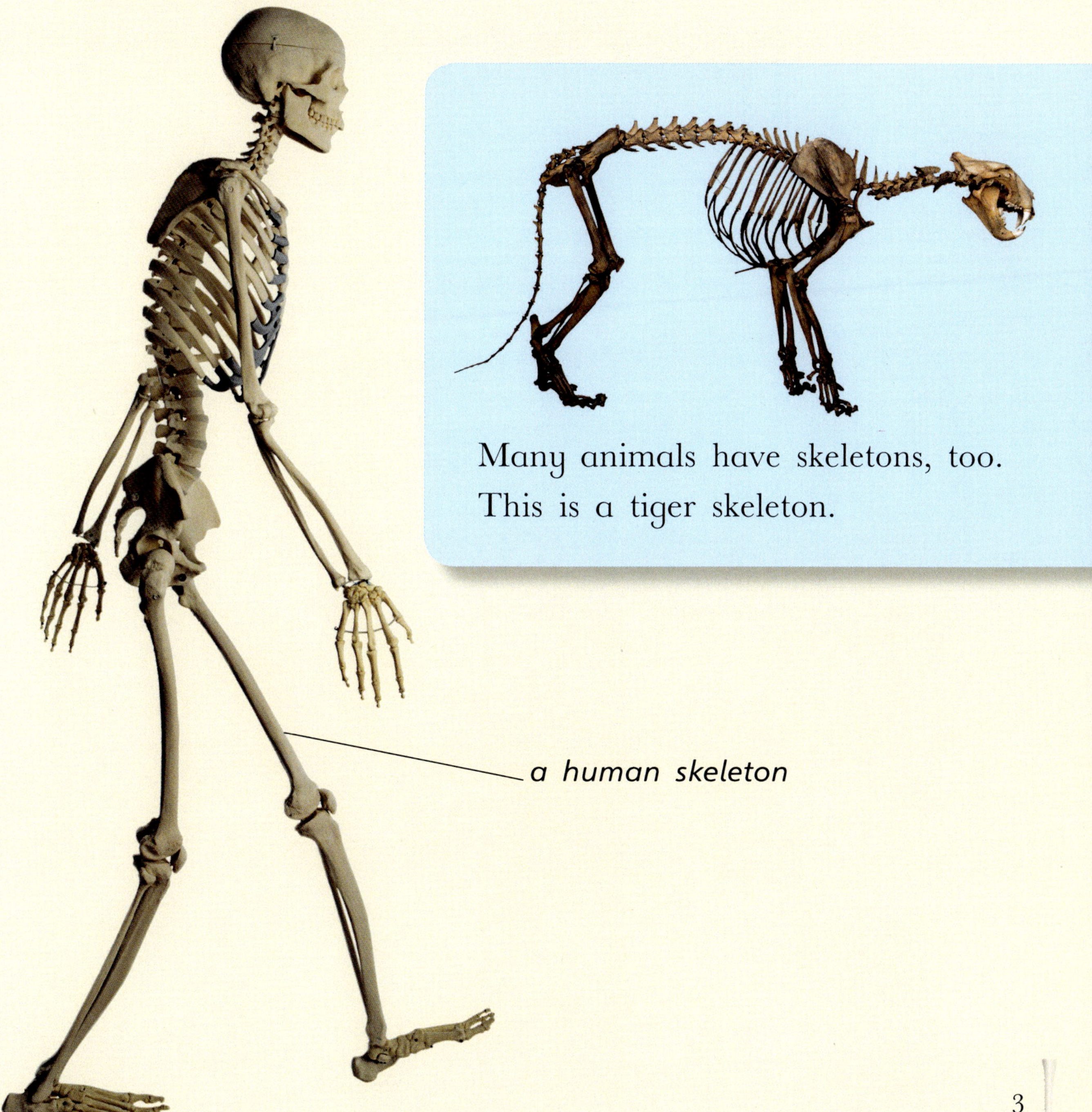

Many animals have skeletons, too.
This is a tiger skeleton.

a human skeleton

How many bones do I have?

An adult has 206 bones.

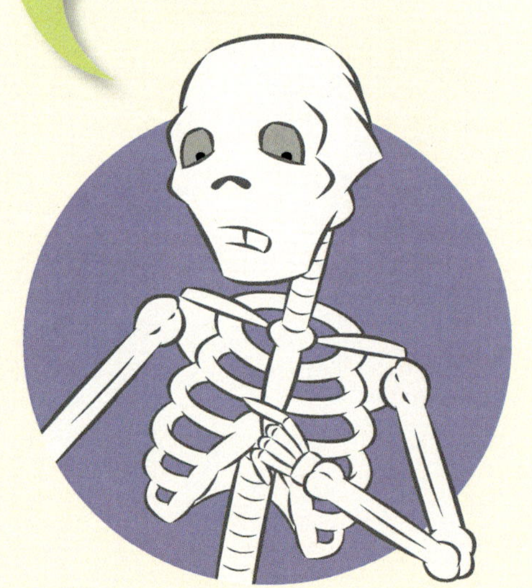

Babies are born with more than 300 bones! When babies grow, some of their bones join together.

Where is the longest bone in my body?

The longest bone is in your leg. It is called the femur (say: *fee-mar*) or the thigh bone.

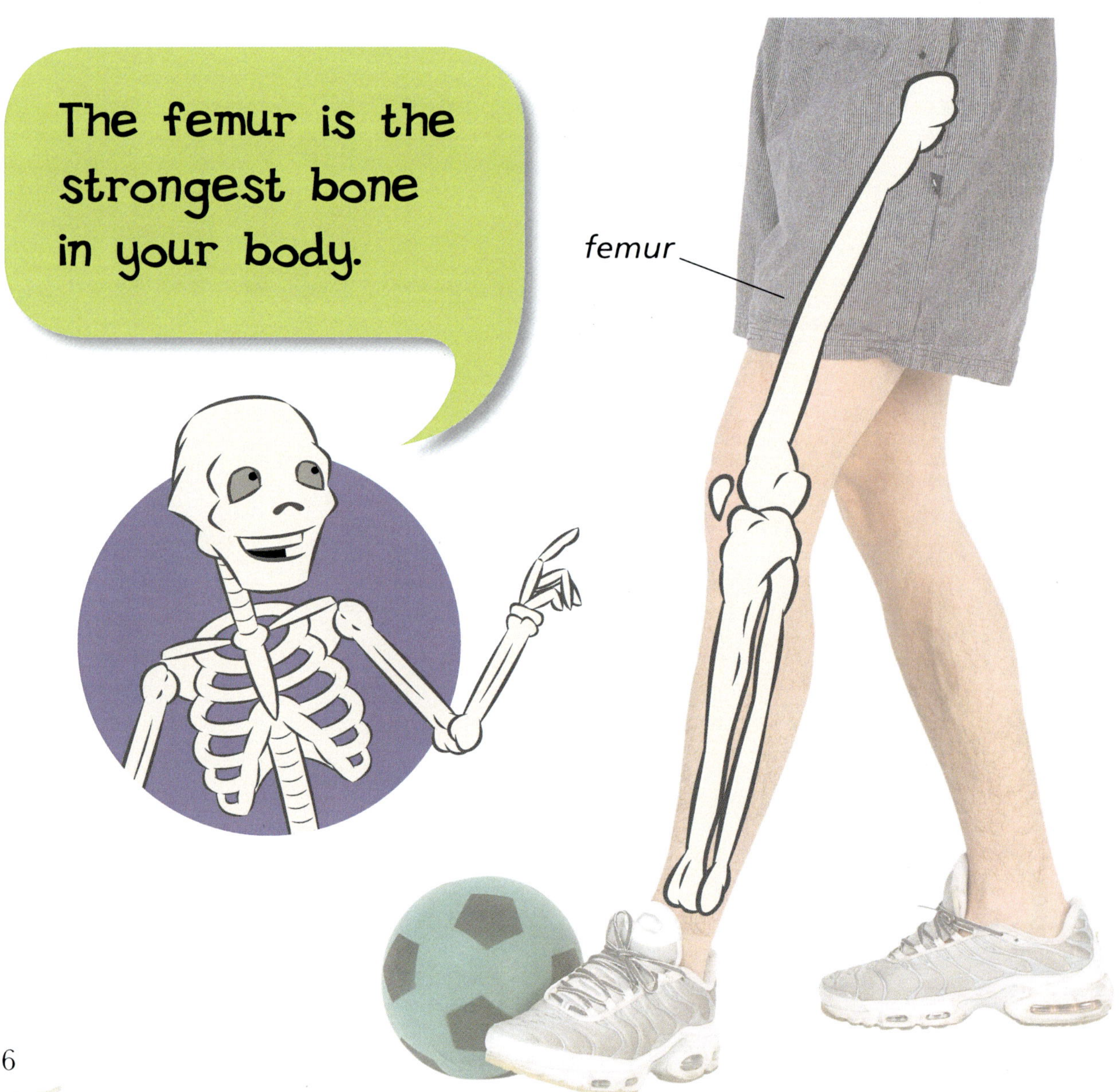

Where is the shortest bone?

The shortest bone is in your ear.
It is called the stapes (say: *stay-pes*) bone.

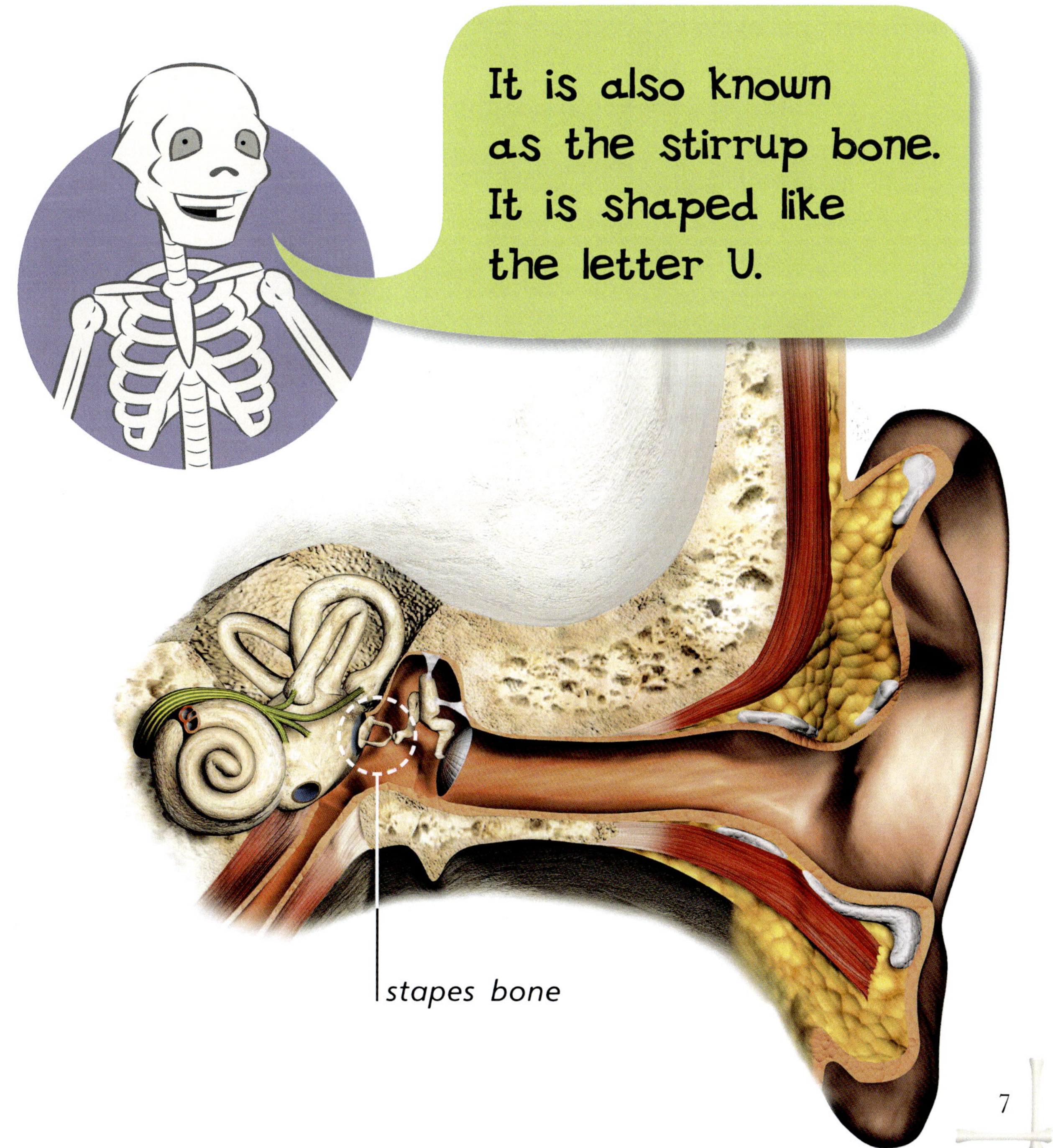

Are there more bones in my hand or in my foot?

There are more bones in your hand.
Each hand has 27 bones.
Each foot has 26 bones.

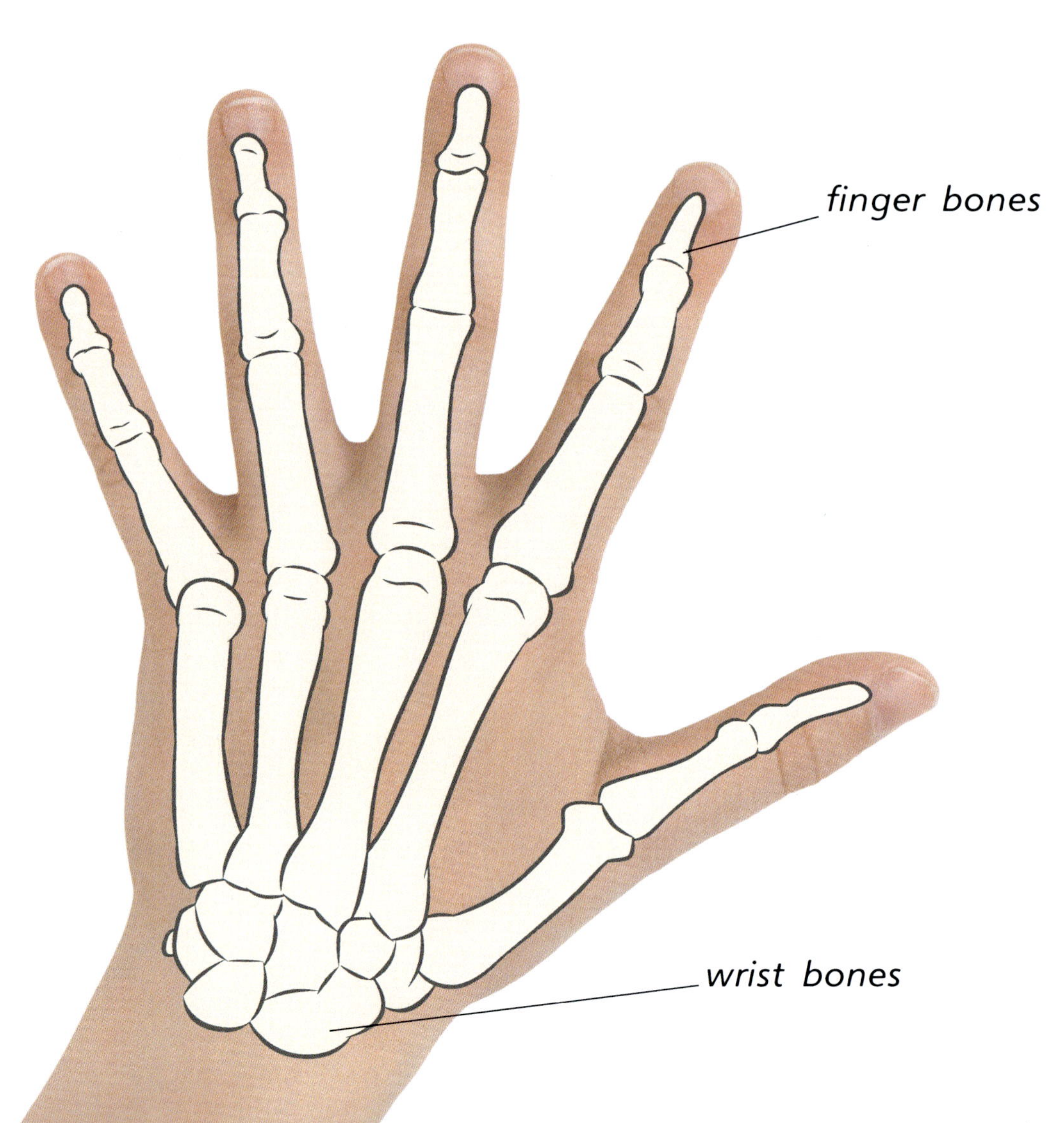

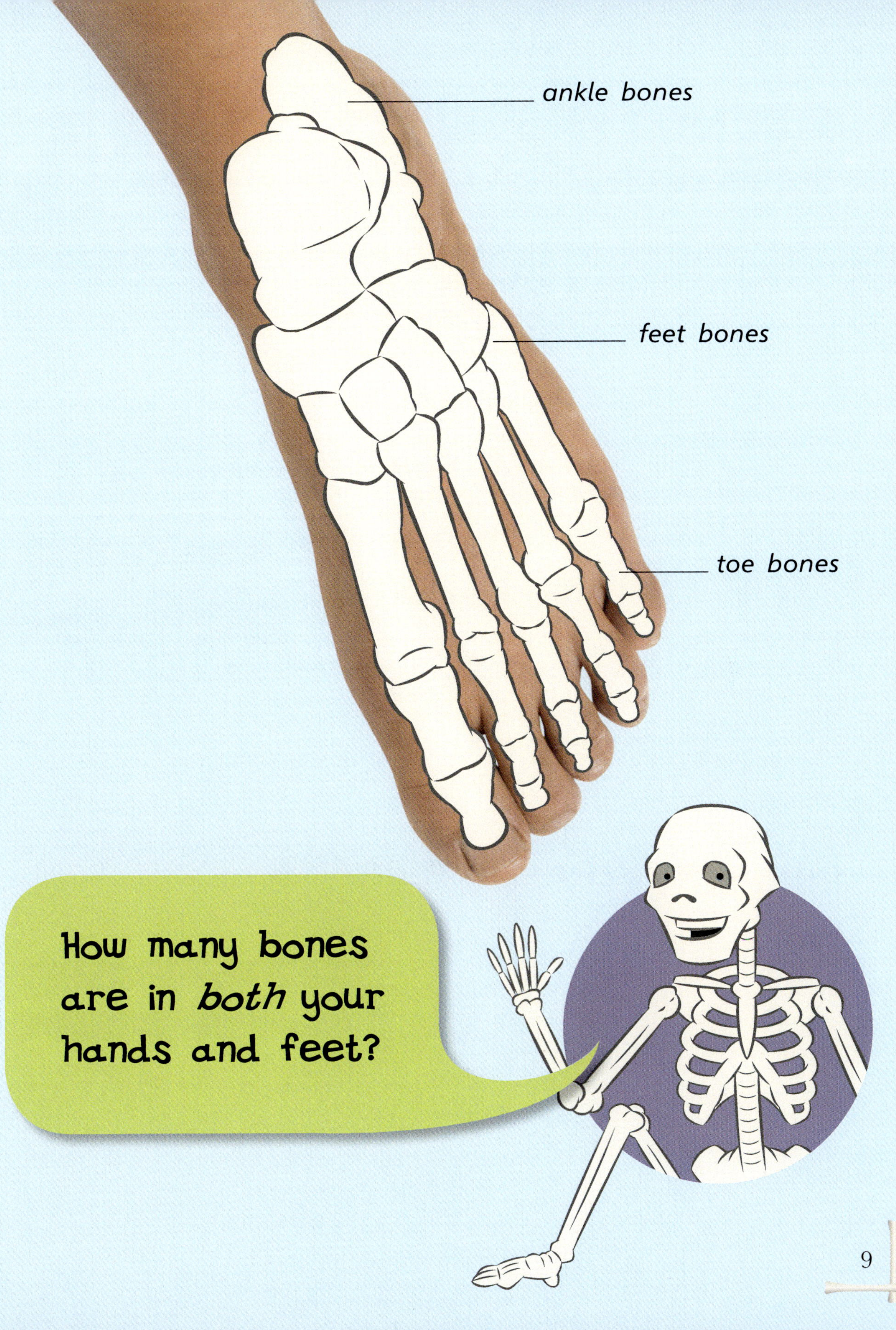
ankle bones
feet bones
toe bones
How many bones are in *both* your hands and feet?

How can I keep my bones strong?

You can help keep your bones strong by eating good food.

Food that is good for your bones:

milk

yoghurt

spinach

cheese

broccoli

Playing sport also keeps your bones strong.

What happens when a bone breaks?

When you break a bone, you have an x-ray. This helps the doctor to see the break.

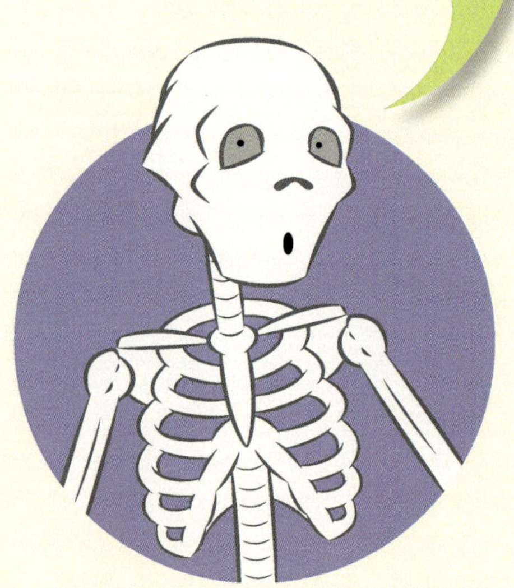

This is an x-ray of a broken arm bone.

Then your broken bone is put into a cast. This will keep your bone very still so it can get better again.

Bones in Your Body

Wow! We found out a lot about bones!

Let's look at how all your bones fit together in your body.

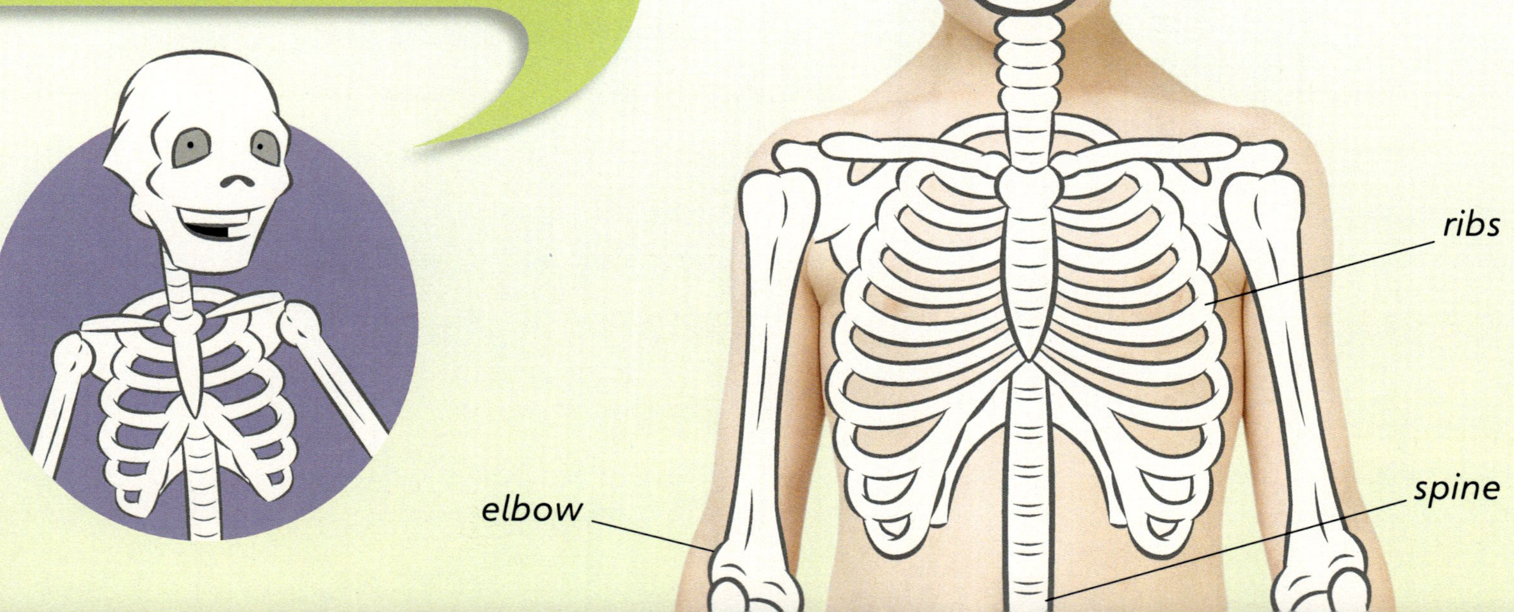

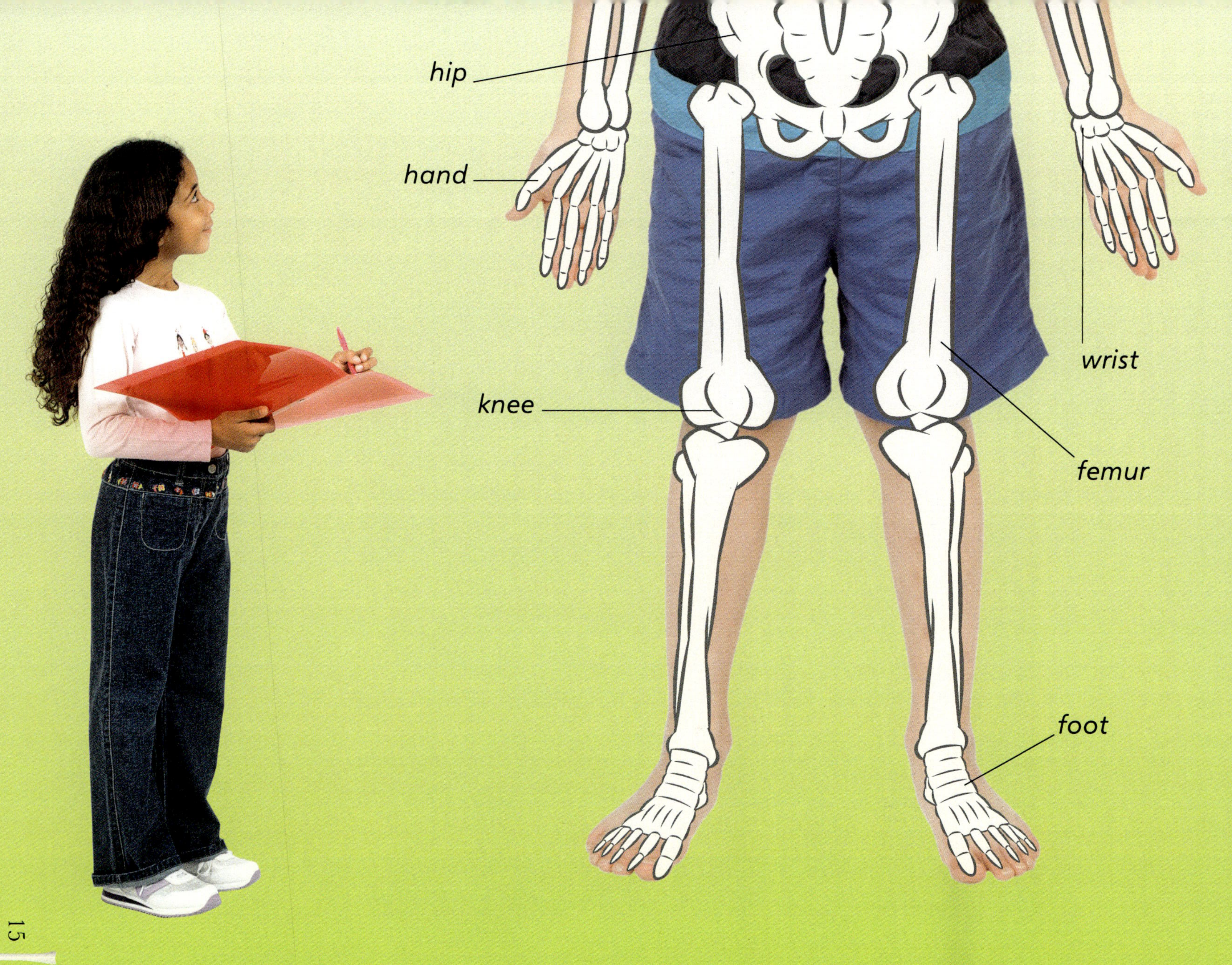
hip
hand
knee
wrist
femur
foot

Index

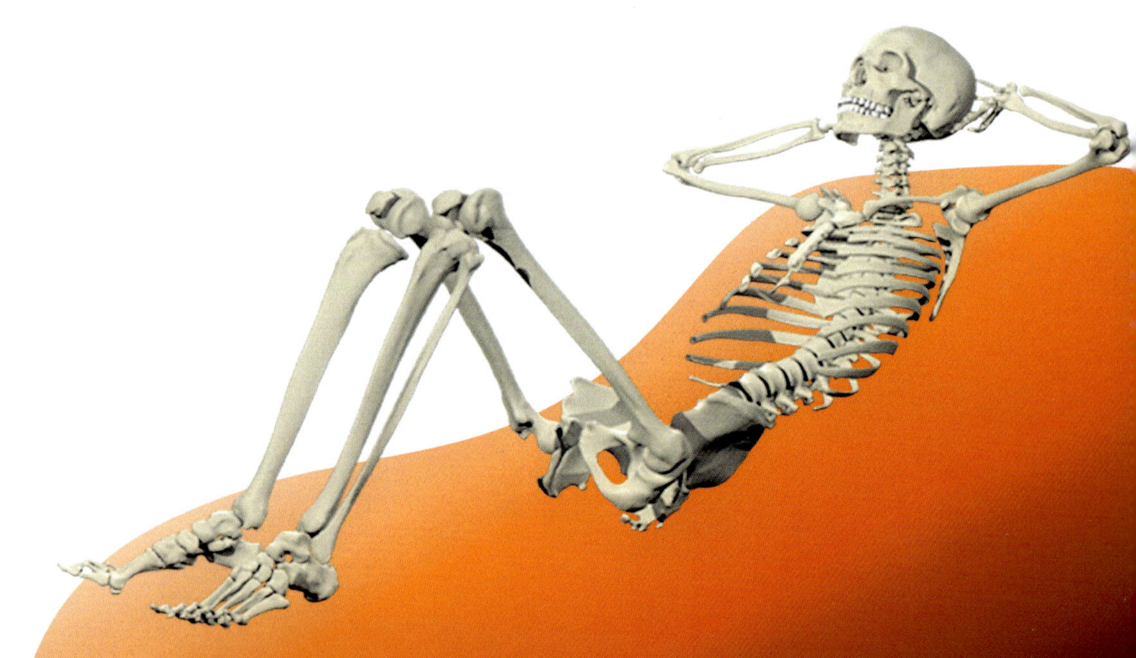